What If?

What If We Run Out of Fossil Fuels?

Kimberly M. Miller

HIGH
interest
books

Children's Press®
A Division of Scholastic Inc.
New York / Toronto / London / Auckland / Sydney
Mexico City / New Delhi / Hong Kong
Danbury, Connecticut

Book Design: Michael DeLisio, Michelle Innes, and Daniel Hosek
Contributing Editor: Matthew Pitt

Library of Congress Cataloging-in-Publication Data

What if we run out of fossil fuels? / Kimberly M. Miller.
    p. cm.
Contents: What are fossil fuels? -- Supply and demand -- Cleaning up the
    environment -- How would your life be different? -- Things you can do.
Summary: Examines mankind's dependence on fossil fuels through scenarios that
    describe life without such items as oil heaters and gasoline-powered cars, and
    describes alternative energy sources and other ways to prepare for this
    possible future.
  ISBN 0-516-23915-5 (lib. bdg.) -- ISBN 0-516-23478-1 (pbk.)
    1. Renewable energy sources--Juvenile literature. 2. Fossil fuels--Juvenile
    literature. [1. Renewable energy sources. 2. Fossil fuels. 3. Power sources.]

TJ808.2 .W47 2002
333.8'2--dc21

                2001047265

CONTENTS

INTRODUCTION

One Saturday morning, you climb out of bed feeling fuzzy, like you've slept too long. Normally your little sister is watching cartoons by now. Today, however, the house is strangely dark and quiet. You hear your father downstairs, but you can't smell the coffee he usually brews at this time.

You look at your watch. You're late! You're supposed to be meeting friends at the mall. You race downstairs to find that the whole house is without electricity. You ask your dad for a ride to the mall. He tells you his car is out of gas.

You run to the bus stop. Thirty minutes later, you're still waiting. Even though the mall is far away, you decide to walk. The street is deserted and creepy. When you arrive, only one friend is waiting—and the mall is closed! "You're the first to get here," she says. "I don't know what happened to the others." The two of you decide the others aren't coming, so you head to the movie theater, about a mile away.

A world without fossil fuels could pitch the planet into some dark days.

   With no buses in sight, you have to walk again. When you arrive, almost an hour later, the movie theater is empty and the doors are locked. "What's going on?" you wonder. "How could all the electricity in my home be off? What would stop the buses from running and even shut down the mall?" All of this could really happen if we ran out of fossil fuels.

CHAPTER ONE

What Are Fossil Fuels?

Millions of years ago, giant swamps covered Earth. Animals and plants lived in them. When these plants and animals died, they sank to the bottom of the swamps. Over many centuries, the decayed remains were covered with layers of dirt that washed into the swamps. Under the weight of the dirt, the decayed remains turned into new things—fossil fuels. Fossil fuels can be found in three different forms. Solid fossil fuel is called coal. Liquid fossil fuel is called petroleum, or oil. Fossil fuels can also exist in a gaseous form. This form is known as natural gas.

Over millions of years, the remains of animals like these brachiosaurs became the stuff fossil fuels are made of.

Why Do We Need Fossil Fuels?

Early in human history, people discovered that they could use fire to stay warm and cook food. Wood and leaves from trees and other plants were probably used as the first fuel. The energy provided by the plants came from the sun. Both plants and animals receive and store energy from the sun. Because of this, fossil fuels also get their energy from the sun. But as fossil fuels formed, the energy became very concentrated, or powerful. This makes fossil fuels burn much hotter and longer than wood.

Some scientists say coal may have been mined in China as early as 1100 B.C. But during the Industrial Revolution in the 1700s, people started using fossil fuels more than ever before. Oil, natural gas, and coal make our lives easier. They give us energy to power

DID YOU KNOW?

If every person on Earth used as much oil and gas as the average American, the world would run out of these fuels in 15 years!

our vehicles and to manufacture, or make, things. They help us make many common items that we use every day.

These three main energy sources power almost everything in your house that whirrs, buzzes, or flicks on and off. The power company that brings light to your bedroom and plays your stereo gets its energy by burning coal or natural gas. Most cars and buses run on gasoline, which is made from oil.

Coal is an invaluable resource, but it is a resource we are running out of.

CHAPTER TWO

Fueling Our World

Fossil fuels are used for more than just powering cars or lighting up houses. Plastic is made from fossil fuels. What would we be forced to give up if we ran out of plastic? Just for starters—the bottles that hold your shampoo, the sandwich bags you put your lunch in, and life-preserving medical equipment. You might even lose the shoes off your feet!

Suppose your mom sends you to the store to pick up a few things. On your list are trash bags, diapers, and ball-point pens. When you get there, you can't find anything on your list! All those items are made of plastic.

That's not all. If we run out of fossil fuels, you won't find lipstick or even lotion in the makeup aisles.

Without plastics, shoppers could walk into supermarkets and find the shelves almost completely bare.

Petroleum jelly, made from oil, is used in making lipsticks and lotions. Even the colors of makeup come from dyes made out of coal.

Are you a sports fan? Think about the equipment you and your favorite players wear during games: Catcher's masks, shin guards, padding, and sneakers are all made with plastic.

FUN FACTS

Plastic helped former New York Yankees star Jimmy Key pitch a winning Game 6 in the 1996 World Series! A torn left rotator cuff had him on the disabled list. Doctors repaired it by inserting plastic stitch anchors into his shoulder bone!

Without fossil fuels, even the world of sports would surely slow down.

Oil or Nothing

If we ran out of fossil fuels right now, we might not be prepared. That's because we've grown to depend on them so much. Right now, 90 percent of the energy used in the United States comes from fossil fuels. This kind of dependency could lead to big problems if we don't have replacement energy sources ready. Scientists expect that Earth's supply of fossil fuels probably won't last much longer. Earth only has fifty to seventy-five years of oil reserves left, and even fewer of natural gas.

If we run out of fossil fuels, our lives could be changed forever. The energy you need for cooking and heat might have to come from a wood-burning stove. You'll probably be in charge of gathering firewood when you get home from school. But what if you live in a city? How will you find wood to heat your house? Even if you have a yard with lots of trees, you might have to compete with neighbors to make sure your family stays warm at night. If energy supplies plummet too far, states may have to worry about blackouts, or temporary losses of electric power.

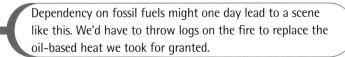

Dependency on fossil fuels might one day lead to a scene like this. We'd have to throw logs on the fire to replace the oil-based heat we took for granted.

The cost of energy will also be affected. In winter 2000, the price of heating oil shot up in New Hampshire. Some families had to cut back on food or medicine just to afford heat through the chilly winter.

Demand for Supply

You may not have to hunt and gather fuel for your family now. But competition for fossil fuels can get fierce. Fossil fuels are not found everywhere. Some countries, such as those in the Middle East, still have large supplies. Some regions in the United States also have fossil fuel supplies. Yet their supply is shrinking. The downtown area of Kilgore, Texas, was once covered with oil wells. People called it "The World's Richest Acre." The wells there are still pumping. However, the oil that was once close to the surface is now much harder to find. After decades of drilling and mining, the supply is vanishing. Fossil fuels are not renewable resources. This means that once they're gone, they can't be replaced.

Like much of the world, the United States now depends on other countries for its energy supply. We buy most of our oil from Middle Eastern nations, such as

Oil wells in states such as Texas used to pump day and night. But once the oil runs dry, it cannot be replaced.

Saudi Arabia, Kuwait, Iran, and Iraq. As a result, these nations are very influential in world politics.

The United States has already faced a serious shortage of fossil fuels. Ask your parents if they remember long lines at gas stations in the 1970s. A trade organization from the Middle East formed during that decade. It was called the Oil Producing and Exporting Countries (OPEC). OPEC worked together to charge higher prices for their oil. In just a few months, gas prices around the world doubled. This created an oil crisis in the United States and Canada.

The crisis made people think about energy conservation, or using less fuel. Car companies began building cars that used less gas. People also learned to use less energy at home. They turned off lights when they weren't home. They ran energy-gobbling appliances, such as dishwashers, less often. In winter, they turned down the heat when they went to bed.

Energy conservation cut down on how much fossil fuel the average person used. But these fuels were still important enough to our economy that the United States went to war to defend its supply. In 1991, Iraq

In the 1970s, staggering costs and supply shortages
made filling up the gas tank a real ordeal.

attacked Kuwait. Iraq also threatened to invade Saudi Arabia. To protect United States allies and their oil supplies, President George Bush commanded the U.S. military to fire missiles at Iraq. With that decision, the Gulf War began.

Anything that puts oil supplies at risk puts the United States at risk. If we don't develop other energy sources, our dependency on fossil fuels could lead to more conflicts. This would result in the highest price of fossil fuels vanishing—loss of human life.

Some think that the United States should try to drill for oil in its own territory. They've proposed drilling in Alaska's Arctic National Wildlife Refuge. Yet some scientists predict that the oil at the refuge would only provide a half-year's worth of fuel. They believe we must think beyond short-term solutions. When it comes to running out of fossil fuels, the question isn't "What if?" but "How soon?"

If the need for fossil fuels leads to war, the consequences will surely be tragic.

CHAPTER THREE

Poisoned Planet

The use of fossil fuels is one of the biggest causes of pollution. Reducing our use of them would benefit our health as well as that of our planet. Natural gas is the cleanest of the three fossil fuel forms. Burning coal releases the most pollutants. But oil spills have devastating effects on the environment. Oil spills have damaged thousands of life forms, some beyond repair.

When fossil fuels burn, they leave behind tiny particles called soot. Burning coal creates a poisonous acid called sulfur dioxide. In London, England, coal smoke from thousands of chimneys flooded the air during the Fatal Fog of 1952. More than four thousand Londoners choked to death as they inhaled the toxic air. After that,

The power that coal provides is often outweighed by the damage it does to the air we breathe.

England passed one of the world's first clean air laws. Cities around the world took notice. Governments took steps to protect their own citizens. In 1970, the U.S. Congress passed the Clean Air Act. This law forced companies to use cleaner fuels and "scrub the air" before sending it out of smokestacks. Now, smokestacks capture the dirty particles before they pollute the air.

Soot can mix with water droplets in the sky to form a brownish-gray haze called smog. In cities such as Los Angeles and Houston, the smog gets so thick it makes it hard to see the skyline. Even the simple act of breathing can be difficult on days when the layer of smog thickens. Wind and rain can carry smog from one state, or even one country, to another!

When sulfur dioxide from smog combines with rain clouds, acid rain is produced. The sulfur dioxide dissolves in the rain and forms sulfuric acid. This acid can kill trees and large groups of fish living in rivers and lakes. Sulfuric acid can also poison our drinking water.

The pollutants in soot and smog can damage human beings, too. They can make asthma worse. They also can cause bronchitis, lung damage, and increase the risk of

New Delhi and other cities all over the world have struggled with the same problems in recent years: soot and smog.

infection. Some experts recently stated that air pollution from burning fossil fuels kills more people than car accidents. They believe that if levels of harmful gases were cut in just four major cities—New York City; Mexico City,

Mexico; São Paulo, Brazil; and Santiago, Chile—sixty-four thousand lives could be saved in the next twenty years!

The Heat Is On

A natural layer of ozone gas covers Earth. It acts as a blanket that lets gases in our atmosphere warm the planet while heat is sent out into space. This blanket also protects humans from the Sun's harmful rays. However, pollution from burning fossil fuels has created a hole in our ozone blanket. This pollution also traps outgoing heat, leading to global warming. Global warming could be the worst long-term effect of burning fossil fuels. It threatens to change Earth's weather patterns. This could lead to massive floods and drought.

World leaders are worried about global warming. In 2000, in Kyoto, Japan, dozens of nations signed a treaty to limit emissions. Emissions are the pollutants that come from factories, power plants, and cars. Following that agreement means conserving fossil fuels and finding alternatives. Developing new sources of energy won't be easy and it won't be cheap. Yet the cost to human life and our planet's health will be far greater if we don't.

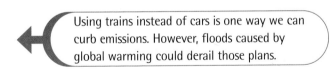

Using trains instead of cars is one way we can curb emissions. However, floods caused by global warming could derail those plans.

CHAPTER FOUR

What Can Be Done?

How would we get around without fossil fuels? Would any cars still run without them? Would you believe putting plants in your gas tank is one alternative? Scientists in Brazil found a way to squeeze the juice from corn and sugar cane to make a fuel called ethanol. At least 26 percent of all car fuel in Brazil has to be made of ethanol. You need a special type of engine for this type of fuel. It burns very cleanly, but not many cars in North America have the engines that run on it.

What if your car ran on batteries? If you live in California, you may already have an electric car! Smog was such a problem there that the state passed a law to cut down on it. By 2003, 10 percent of cars sold in the

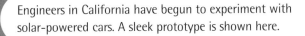

Engineers in California have begun to experiment with solar-powered cars. A sleek prototype is shown here.

state will be zero emissions vehicles (ZEVs). This means they won't send any soot into the air. But even if you had a ZEV, you'd still be out of luck if we lost our fossil fuels! Electric cars have to be plugged in at night. If the coal-fueled power plant shuts down, so does your car.

Home Cooking

What kind of energy would keep your house comfortable without fossil fuels? Solar energy, or energy from the sun, might help. Scientists can catch this energy in panels they call solar cells. Some solar cells store just enough energy to give off heat for a water heater and a few rooms. Others change heat into electricity. But using solar cells to catch power from the sun uses a lot of land. Today, a solar power plant that produces 100 megawatts can cover up to one square mile! Yet such a plant would be able to power only about 100,000 houses.

How about using wind or water for clean, cheap energy? People have been pumping water with windmills for hundreds of years. Lately, scientists have found ways to make that power stronger. In the high, windy hills of Northern California, you might be surprised to see a

Solar power is a renewable form of energy that doesn't pollute. Its main drawback is that it demands a lot of land.

wind farm. There, hundreds of windmills turn together to make electricity.

You can also make electricity using water. Hydroelectric power concentrates the energy of a flowing river by sending it through a dam. When the water is released through a narrow passage, pressure is created. This pressure turns turbines, which in turn produces electricity. However, wind and water power plants take up at least as much space as solar power plants. And usually, they provide only a small part of the energy needed. Hydroelectric power can also cause bigger problems. Governments sometimes have flooded out whole forests or towns to get enough water to make power.

Is there any place where life would be the same if we ran out of fossil fuels? In India and Brazil, you could still have light and electricity in your home. That's because these nations already use lots of hydroelectric energy. Some places in the United States near wide, fast rivers use hydroelectric power, too. If you are one of the eight million people served by the Tennessee Valley Authority, you could still have some power at home. This mega-power company has nearly thirty hydroelectric dams.

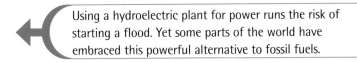

Using a hydroelectric plant for power runs the risk of starting a flood. Yet some parts of the world have embraced this powerful alternative to fossil fuels.

DID YOU KNOW?

It takes a million years to produce the amount of fossil fuel that the people of Earth use in one year!

In the United States, each state decides what part of its budget to spend on technology. California is very creative at finding new sources of power. In sunny Southern California, there are large solar plants outside of Los Angeles, San Diego, and San Francisco. About 10 percent of the world's supply of wind power comes from California. But if your state doesn't spend time and money looking for new fuel sources, you could be completely without power.

This new technology is exciting and promising. But nothing can replace what fossil fuels do today. Most of us use some type of fossil fuel to travel, light and heat our homes, or do our work. Before fossil fuels run out, we must find better ways to use the clean, cheap power we get from wind, water, and the sun. It's a race against time.

For some towns, the answer to the fossil fuel problem is blowing in the wind.

Running on Empty

This chart shows how much energy certain appliances gobble up. Make sure to turn off appliances like your TV or stereo when you leave the house. If you do, Earth won't be running on empty.

Amount of Energy

Clock radio   Radio   TV   Coffee maker   Dishwasher

CHAPTER FIVE

You've Got the Answer

We should make plans for life after fossil fuels. But are there choices you can make now to slow down our use of fossil fuels? Absolutely.

At Home

How many times do you leave the room and leave your stereo on? If there's no one around to hear it, turn it off! The same goes for the lights and the TV. Think about how many appliances are running in your house all the time. The refrigerator, clocks, phones, maybe even a computer! All these small items put together use a lot of energy we can't afford to lose.

Energy may be escaping from your house as you read this book! If there are gaps around your doors and windows, you're not only heating or cooling the air inside your house. You're letting that air escape outside, too. If you have this problem, you can take steps to solve it. Roll up a towel to place at the base of the window or door. If your house is extremely cold in the winter and hot in the summer, you may need new insulation. Talk to your family about finding a plan that will help you save energy.

Find ways to save gas, too. For short trips, don't take the car. Walk if possible, or take a bus or train. Some trains use six times less energy than cars. And trains can hold dozens of passengers, not just a few, like a car. When you or your family buy a new car, remember to check the gas mileage. Some cars get up to 40 miles (64 kilometers) per gallon. But others get as little as 10 (16 km)!

Community Action

Look around your neighborhood. You will find lots of ways to help your neighbors learn to cut back on using fossil fuels. At school, why not suggest to your science teacher that your class do a project on fossil fuel conservation? You can talk about the results at a local Earth Day event.

Does your city recycle? Call your local sanitation department and ask. If your town doesn't recycle, find out why. Recycling saves fossil fuels by reusing plastics.

If we don't recycle our plastic bottles, it could have a landslide effect on our planet's fossil fuel supply.

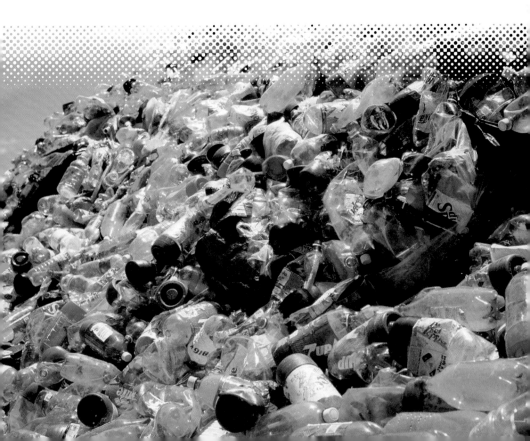

You can talk to neighbors about why your city needs to recycle. Lots of ordinary people have started recycling programs across the country!

Ask your parents to find out if your state has an energy conservation program. Some cities only buy police cars and buses that have high gas mileage. This saves money and fossil fuels. Keep in touch with your state representatives. Learn about new laws on the production and use of fossil fuels. Does your representative have a good conservation record? If so, volunteer to help out with his or her campaign.

Long Term Plan

Your role in saving our supply of fossil fuels doesn't have to end there. Stay up to date. Look for information about fuels in the news. Read the newspaper to learn about alternative energy, and where our fuels are coming from.

If you're really interested, plan a career that makes you part of the solution. Work with a company that develops new fuels. You could design and build cars that run on cleaner energy sources. Or you could work for city or state programs that help people insulate their homes properly.

By writing to our nation's leaders, we can make sure they realize that we take energy conservation seriously.

It's impossible to predict the exact moment when we'll run out of fossil fuels. But the day is definitely coming. The best policy is to be ready as soon as possible. That way, we won't literally be left in the dark when we do run out. It won't shock us like it did in the 1970s. And it won't force a huge change in our lifestyle, or lead to war. If we all conserve our energy resources and keep looking for new ones, your kids might not have to fear a world without fossil fuels.

allies friendly nations

concentrated very powerful, or a high amount

conservation the act of reducing how much energy a person or nation uses

efficient to work or run as smoothly as possible

emissions pollutants that escape from cars, factories, and power plants

ethanol a type of fuel made from corn and sugar cane

fossil fuels types of fuel that come from the remains of plants and animals

hydroelectric energy power that is produced by rushing water

insulation material that stops air from escaping a building

manufacture to make something

petroleum oil

renewable resources fuel sources that can be reused over time, such as wind, water, or the Sun

smog a mixture of smoke and fog; a haze of pollution that forms when soot mixes with water droplets

solar cells panels that can catch the sun's energy and turn it into electricity

watts a unit of measurement for electrical energy

wind farm a place where hundreds of windmills turn in unison to produce electricity

ZEVs Zero Emissions Vehicles; clean-running vehicles that do not send polluting gases into the air when they run

FOR FURTHER READING

Chandler, Gary and Kevin Graham. *Alternative Energy Sources.* New York, NY: Henry Holt & Company, 1996.

Gibson, Michael. *The Energy Crisis.* Vero Beach, FL: Rourke Enterprises, Inc., 1987.

Graham, Ian S. *Fossil Fuels, Vol. 1.* Austin, TX: Raintree/Steck-Vaughn Publishers, 1999.

Parker, Steve and Edward Parker. *Fuels for the Future, Vol. 2.* Austin, TX: Raintree/Steck-Vaughn Publishers, 1998.

Snedden, Robert. *Energy from Fossil Fuels.* Crystal Lake, IL: Heinemann Library, 2001.

Web Sites

Natural Resources Defense Council—Features
http://www.nrdc.org/features/default.asp
Check out the "Environmental Timeline" feature on this Web site. You can scroll across the timeline to uncover Earth's environmental wins and losses in the last thirty years. It includes everything from Earth Day to the oil crisis to the Clean Air Act.

Citizens for Renewable Energy (CFRE)
http://www.web.ca/~cfre/
This site provides information and photographs on alternative sources of energy. This Canadian group's mission is to reduce the use of fossil fuels, and to increase our use of renewable resources.

RESOURCES

Alliance to Save Energy
http://www.ase.org/
This site features lots of information on how energy can be used more efficiently—right now! It also provides articles on current energy problems, such as city blackouts. Check out the link for Green Schools, a program to cut down on energy waste.

American Plastics Council—Plastics in Your Life
http://www.americanplasticscouncil.org/benefits/ in_your_life/in_your_life.html
This page describes the connections between plastics, cars, space exploration, athletic performance, and good health.

INDEX

INDEX

About the Author

Kimberly M. Miller grew up in the oil patch town of Kilgore, Texas, where she learned about the sights and smells of fossil fuels. Studying the environment at Hendrix College and the University of Texas taught her about the risky side of depending on coal, oil, and natural gas. She now spends her days as a city planner in New York City.